Locked In
SECOND EDITION

Poetry by Barbara Randall and Erika DeBarros

Illustrated by Kira Brant

Creative Literature Division
www.TheCultureConnection.com

Published by The Culture Connection
www.TheCultureConnection.com
orders@TheCultureConnection.com

Copyright © 2002 by Barbara Randall and Erika DeBarros

All rights reserved. No part of this book may be reproduced or utilized in any form or by any means, electronic or mechanical, including photocopying, recording or by any information storage or retrieval system, without permission in writing from the Publisher.

Inquiries should be emailed to: orders@TheCultureConnection.com.

ISBN 0-9712383-0-8
Library of Congress Control Number: 2005937289

First Printing 2002
Second Printing 2005
Third Printing 2008

Printed in the United States of America

Illustrations by Kira Brant

"To Phil, my only son for believing in me and giving me the strength to believe in myself."
— Barbara Randall

"For Pierre and Caleb."
— Erika DeBarros

"To Aunt Lutherine, for having the strength to step out of the fog and inspiring us to do the same."
— Barbara & Erika

PARTNERS IN THE JOURNEY...
Part One

Barbara Randall. *Where do I begin? She is a dozen people and one and not because of her illness. When I first met Ms. Randall she seemed bereft of word, thought and feeling. She appeared opaque, a muddy pool with no reflection; one I could not see through.*

In knowing her for nearly five years, I find I was wrong. She is not as the color black, absorbing all light and giving none back. She is instead a full spectrum, composed of all things, reflecting and refracting light brilliantly; so much so that I was blinded.

She had so many talents, so many feelings, so many fears and hopes and dreams and nightmares that she was often mute. But oh, could she sing. She sang out all that she couldn't say and inflected her music with the emotions that she dared not show. Now her voice finds another path. Ms. Randall is bearing her soul in her writings. You hear her voice resonant with emotion and conviction as much in this poetry as you did when hearing a song soar from her lips.

As with any artist, this work comes from Mrs. Randall's heart, her mind, her history. But it encompasses a broad range of experiences and feelings that any of us can relate to or at least understand. I hope to keep hearing her sing for a long time, in one way or another.

— Carmen McIntyre, M.D

Part Two

Four years ago, I met a beautiful woman who was frightened, talented and depressed. Her very being appeared to be a collection of contradictions. She moved through life seemingly unaware of many of the realities of the world and her own situation. Over the course of the following four years, I became aware of her many other talents and bizarre behaviors. I would later learn these were features of the alternate personalities of this complex woman.

Throughout this time, as her therapist, I have been privileged to travel with her on her journey towards mental health and self-development. Many words could describe this journey. Courageous seems to be the most fitting. In order to overcome the many effects of her pain and illness she has navigated through a maze of memories of abuse, neglect and manipulation, that created the bonds that have shackled her mind, body and spirit.

It has not been an easy or steady journey. During this time, she has learned of painful and difficult aspects of her life, of which she has been consciously unaware. But her resolve has remained. She has made progress in rebuilding her life into one that is more aware of the realities of the past and the present and one that holds hope for a brighter future.

There are miles yet to travel on this personal sojourn. This book of poetry is a significant milestone of that journey. It has been a tool to declare the knowledge she has gained and the emotions she continues to learn to express. It is also a gift she has wanted to give to others who choose to take their own journey of healing.

— Michele Bietler, MSN, RN, NP, CS

The Troops
The Personalities of Barbara Randall

Barbara Randall (Babs)
Host Self. Singer/Songwriter. Barbara has 3 children and 5 grandchildren and goes by the nickname Babs. She married and had her first child at age 16.

The Babies (Babsie & Babsie-Wabsie)
They are both between 3—5 years old. Born during early childhood. Babsie-Wabsie cannot speak above a whisper. They are both very traumatized and still live in fear.

Liz
She is 17-years old, streetwise, rough around the edges and prone to fights. Liz carries many childhood memories.

Aurelia Curry
Aurelia is in her early 20's. She was born early in marriage. Came to help raise children and deal with marriage. Aurelia Curry is extremely intelligent and loves to dance.

Aurelia 2
Her age is unknown but she is believed to be younger than Aurelia Curry. She was born to physically give birth to Barbara's children. Aurelia 2 is now asleep.

Amelia
Amelia is also in her early 20's and she was born around the same time as Aurelia Curry. Amelia rarely comes out and her function is still unknown.

Barbara 1
She is in her late 30's, nurturing, calm, admired and respected by the other troops. She speaks French and spends her free time reading dictionaries, encyclopedias and the bible. Barbara 1 was born after the host Barbara's wedding.

Barbara 2
She is in her late 40's. Born shortly after Barbara 1. Of all the troops, Barbara 1 and Barbara 2 appear to be closest to the host Barbara in personality. Barbara 2 is very serious and also speaks French.

Barbara Coleman
Barbara Coleman is in her late 30's. She sings jazz, and has performed in several musicals and reviews. She is a glamorous larger than life diva who loves to perform. Born after the host Barbara separated from her husband's band.

Bobbie
Bobbie is in her late 20's. She is from the islands and speaks with a slight accent. Bobbie handles disputes and financial matters. She must hide her accent when she comes out.

G.
G. is 17 years old and confused about his gender. He loves shopping and playing with the grandchildren. He makes people listen to Barbara and has a quick temper.

Mad Girl
She refuses to give her real name. She is in her late 20's. Mad Girl carries the anger. She considers herself to be the protector.

The Quiet Ones
Their ages are unknown. They do not communicate with anyone on the outside yet. Their function is also still unknown.

The Boys
The Boys are in their late teens. The fighters. They consider themselves "the men" and take care of things "girls can't do."

Elizabeth
Elizabeth's age is still unknown. She is shy and timid, innocent, sweet and desperately wants to study the bible.

The Newcomer
Unknown age. She has no idea why she's here. She was born in a courtroom in the mist of a traumatic divorce. Has only minimal communication with the other troops. It is believed that she will become the complete Barbara Randall after all the troops join together.

Introduction
by Barbara Randall

"I had four children to raise"
"I told him to stop"
"He was the love of my life"
"My conscience is clear"
"God is on my side!"

How could any woman, with small children in her home, marry a suspected pedophile?

Jacob Walters, the man my mother was dating, was rumored to be a pedophile. During their courtship, Mama was told about the rumors. She was told, "He just wants to be close to your little girls." Mama chose to ignore those rumors and bring Jacob Walters into our lives. We were perfect prey for this demented man with free reign to satisfy insatiable appetites for perversion.

My nightmare began in the cold damp basement of a rented house, in Indianapolis, Indiana, in the mid-1950s. I was not yet afraid of basements. I was not yet afraid of the dark and I was not yet afraid of the big man we would soon call Daddy.

When Jacobs's large hands lifted me until my tiny legs dangled in the air and the cold, hard metal from some unknown surface rudely chilled my bottom, that didn't frighten me either. But when his fingers parted my legs and poked deeply into my body until I felt pain, I learned fear. I remember that I cried and as Jacob Walters tried to calm me, he gently cautioned me not to tell.

The abuse very quickly became a pattern and his gentle counsel became a harsh warning that rang loud and clear. My fear and confusion increased.

Gradually, myriads of mysterious phobias and strange behaviors were born, rooted in that dark cellar. These phobias and strange behaviors emerged to bewilder and confound me and to label me peculiar for decades to come.

Like a scene from a movie, I remember when my sister and I told Mama that Jacob was bothering us. Bothering is the first word that comes to mind when I think of the abuse. After years of therapy, I still struggle to remind myself that what Daddy did to me was more than just a bother. After years of therapy, still I'm unable to gaze easily into the fact that my stepfather raped me.

Mama knew what we meant. She knew that we had been touched sexually; that we had been hurt sexually. She asked me and I told her, "yes, he's bothering me, too." Years later, Mama told me that when she confronted Jacob about the abuse, "he foamed at the mouth and his eyes glazed over." Still, his quick denial of the accusation comforted her to the point of false belief and eventual denial of it all.

Later, when Daddy came for me, he was angry. His voice had a rough edge that I'd never heard before and I was afraid. He never had seemed angry before. He had told me not to tell. He said Mama wouldn't believe me. He said it wouldn't do any good. He said that Mama would be hurt and angry. He had been right.

I never told Mama again or anyone else. The subject was never mentioned again and the remarkable process of repression began. I crossed the threshold of hopelessness. I knew that I was alone, unloved and unlovable. The perception that I am unlovable persists to this day, fostered by Mama's declaration that I did it willingly. That it was my fault and that he bought me for the price of, "two White Castle hamburgers."

The first of my troops came. A small girl, like me, called Babsie. She could not speak above a whisper and she lived in perpetual fear. She could not catch her breath and had trouble breathing. She still does. The unbearable weight of Daddy's body has forever forced the breath from her lungs.

Soon, another child came, another little girl, called Babsie-Wabsie. She had to come because Babsie needed help and I was nowhere to be found. It was these two young girls, my infantile allies, who watched in numbed silence as my mother took the hand of Jacob Walters in Holy Matrimony, promising to love, honor and obey him, forsaking all others, putting no one above him, 'til death do us part.'

Mama fulfilled that vow to her husband and Jacob raped me at will, until, around age thirteen, my body matured to the point that it no longer attracted him. Until that time, I endured his attentions in silence. His rape was brutal and complete. There was pain and penetration and now, I remember it vividly.

I remember school days, when noontime meant that out of my three siblings, I alone was taken home for a quick lunch and quick sex with Daddy before afternoon classes.

I remember the sinister shadows on my bedroom walls at night that would materialize into human form and carry me off to the torture chamber that was my mother's bed. I remember praying that someone would know, that someone would simply guess the secret I couldn't tell. I spoke telepathically, through the sadness in my eyes, but no one ever heard. And strange behaviors, like the layers of shorts I wore under my clothes, were tell-tale signs that no one could decipher.

This was the first chapter of my life. It ended when I met Peter Collins, got pregnant and was forced to marry him at the age of sixteen. Peter read me like a book. He knew that I was scarred and fractured; perfect prey. He built on the dismal foundation that my parents had laid.

Peter rubbed salt into all my open wounds and inflicted new ones of his own. He began an incredible campaign of violence, intimidation and psychological warfare that escalated to fever pitch over a period of some thirty years.

We spent our wedding night in a transient hotel. A mentally challenged girl, no older than I, sobbed in the lobby, begging to go home. We ended up in the room next to hers. Through the paper-thin walls, I heard her terrified screams as her 'date' forced himself on her. I was crying, too, for myself and for her.

Life in Peter's domain was an existence of torture, peppered with unexpected acts of benevolence, which kept me off-guard and constantly confused. His mind was a cesspool of diabolical plots and schemes. His power was awesome and complete. His temper could build to volcanic eruption with split-second speed. He would beat me and then surprise me with a car.

He made passes at my friends and paraded an endless array of strange women before me, while he professed undying love for me. I was not allowed to work, to voice, or even to have an opinion. I was forbidden to question him on any matter; yet he praised me for my brilliance.

He convinced me that I was skinny, bucked-toothed and that no one else would ever want me. He hated my laugh and in time, I learned to stifle it until it disappeared altogether.

He told me and anyone else who would listen, that I was sexless, frigid and abhorred intimacy. Still, he invoked 'the five second rule', which gave me five seconds to look at any man before incurring a blow to the face. Most of my beatings were due to my 'flagrant flirtations' with men. If a man flirted with me, I still got the beating, because I "must have done something to encourage him."

I found myself flinching dramatically, covering my face with my hands whenever Peter passed by me. I learned to look down or to the side, when any man was in sight, never risking eye contact. To this day, loud noises and sudden movements cause me to jump out of my skin.

My inherent fear of anger intensified to the point of immobilization. The very thought, the notion, that Peter might become angry, terrified me. Insomnia, panic attacks, eating disorders, obsessions and compulsions took over. More and more, I began to know that I was losing time and to fear that I was losing my mind.

Unrelenting depression, deep, dark and painful beyond words, engulfed me. I had no ability to defend or protect myself and worse, I was incapable of protecting my children.

One horrible day when Erika, my oldest child, was fourteen years old, I sent my children to school and swallowed several bottles of pain pills. Erika came home from school in time to watch her father carry my lifeless body away saying, "look what you've done, you've killed your mother."

I spent a month in the hospital and my children spent a month home alone, forbidden to say a word to anyone. This was no mere cry for help; I wanted to die very badly. That first attempt at ending my life would be followed by other ones, more drastic and more severe.

To this day, after over ten years of hospitalizations and treatment, I continue to suffer the ill effects of sexual, physical and psychological abuses that began in childhood. I still suffer from night terrors, which leave me unable to sleep for weeks at a time. I have spent months in jail and even awakened one day to find myself in a tree an hour from my home.

It was only after all of this that the mayhem dominating my life was finally given a name, Multiple Personality Disorder, now known as Dissociative Identity Disorder. Then, I was slowly introduced to my Troops; the various personalities who lived inside me, those who fought, suffered, grew and in some cases died for me. I came to know these individuals. Some proved to be my allies and some were resentful enemies.

There were frightened children, angry teenagers and weary young women. I was fascinated with the range of fears, hopes, talents and accomplishments unique to each of my Troops. They called "themselves" Troops because Troops, they were. An invisible army; powerful in its resolve to protect its own.

The most painful part of my life remains the legacy, the inheritance I left to my children. They watched my abuse at the hands of a hateful husband. They suffered abuse in many forms as I watched in muted horror.

I was lost in a thickening fog, unable to show deep emotion. I was distanced from those who were closest to my heart; the innocent children I brought into my troubled world; two beautiful, gifted, vulnerable girls and a darkly brilliant, deep-thinking boy who only sees life in shades of black and gray.

As they reached out for me, I was retreating more deeply into that numbing fog. Soon, their mother, their only conceivable means of protection, was utterly lost to them. And then, they were alone, without a mother to be there for them and with a father who should not have been.

— Barbara Randall

Locked In, Part One
by Erika DeBarros

Can You Help Me Find My Mother? 24
Her Family 25
The Grandmother 26
Queen Evil 27
Still 28
Seeds 29
Moods 30
Lost Mind 32
Night Terrors 33
The Girl In My Mind 34
Winter Kills 35
Cocaine 36
The Law Is Divine 37
Cry 38
Spanking 39
Tick 40
Daddy 41
Images 42
Mirror, Mirror 43
Crazy Black Curls 44
Father 45
His Rational 46
Separation 47
Father's Reward 48
Locked In 50
A Prayer For Forgiveness 51
Praise 52

Cold Drink 53
Hope 54
Waste Of Time 55
Shut Up 56
Nobody Knows, One 57
Nobody Knows, Two 57
Dead Men Tell No Tales 58
White Washed Grave 59
Destiny 60
Moving On 61
Marriott Midnights 62
The Greatest Gift 64
Truce 65

Locked In, Part Two
by Barbara Randall

Have You Seen My Little Girl?	70
Men Deceive	71
Erika	72
Hope, II	73
Nature's Spotlight	74
Retrospect	76
Tisha	77
Impotence	78
The Five-Second Rule	79
Laugh	80
The Tyrant	81
Fantasy	82
Reality	82
Insanity	83
Compromise	84
Exasperation	85
Incest	86
Pandora's Box	88
Casualties Of War	89
Part 1, Casualty Of War	89
Part 2, Legacy	89
Part 3, Her Way	90
Vexation	92
Despicable Sin	93
Locked In, II	94
Questions	96
My Wish	97
Shackles	98

Sinking	99
Dreams	100
Hissy Fit	101
Inside Suicide	102
Depression	104
Mitigation	105
Our Poem	106
Memories	107
Island Girl	108
Island Dream	109
No Vacancy	110
Lessons	112
Multiples	113
Alone In The Trenches	114
Ignorance Is Mean	115
Peter's Song	116
Pain	118
The Grass Is Always Greener	119
Lime Green Dress	120
Too Late	121
Consequence	122
Funny	123
Fate	124
There's A Baby On Your Hip	125
Ode To Alice	126
When Butchie Died	128
For The Pumpkins	129
Mama's Sisters	130

Tears 131
For The Grandparents 132
A Little Girls Eyes 134
A Soft Place To Fall 137
Credulity 138
Your Husband 139
Charlatan 140
Wanton 141
Think 142
Irony 143
Time 144
Don't Ask 146
I Can't Tell You 147
Affirmation 148
Dilemma 149
Attitude 150
Forgiveness 152
My Time To Heal 154
Closure 155
Healing 158
What Is Dissociative Identity Disorder (DID)? 160
How Does A Dissociative Disorder Develop? 161
Can Dissociative Disorders Be Cured? 162
How Do I Get More Information? 163

PART ONE

Locked In, Part One
by Erika DeBarros

Locked In, One
The Preface

The moment my mother told me that she had multiple personalities is forever frozen in my mind. Memories flashed and flew into place, finally completing the puzzle that was my childhood. The news however, was not a shock, for I have always known, at least on some level that my mother was more than one. Deep down I knew that other parents didn't disappear for days or weeks at a time; coming and going without a word. I knew that other mothers always looked at their children with recognition and could always call them by their names. I fully understood why sometimes I was the parent and she was the child.

I remember the mother who patiently helped me with my homework and the one who would tuck me in bed. I remember the one who would turn the whole house into a giant playground and the one who seemed to wish I were dead. I could, in that instance, forgive her for becoming a human punching bag for my father and for staring so blankly and mutely when he focused his attention on me.

I soon learned of the venomous abuses she suffered throughout her entire childhood, under the jealous eyes of her mother. I realized that only someone as brilliant as my mother could have found a way to survive by fragmenting into different selves; cleverly assigning a secret holding place for each emotion and skill, skills that could be recalled when she needed them with the quickness of a keystroke.

I now appreciate the power of the human mind and spirit. I find myself awed by The Troops, my mother's enigmatic allies and the protectors of her sanity. I'm still learning all the

Part One

different parts of my mother and although I do not know all of them by name, I am able to embrace them all, learn from them and grow with them. I hope that I am able to become such an inspiration for my own children. I hope to show them the fighting spirit of my mother, so that they, too, can find their own way to survive in this world, so they can be happy and healthy and most importantly, whole.

— *Erika DeBarros*

Locked In

Can You Help Me Find My Mother?

I know she's in there somewhere.
I can feel her need me,
lost behind your icy stare.
I think that you can help me,
but you will not share your clues.
Now, I am left alone
as you attempt to fill her shoes.

I fear I've never known her,
never had a mother to hold.
Though you look something like her,
your touch is faux and cold.
I know you've seen my mother.
Is she anything like me?
Do I remind you of her
or of the one who made her leave?

I know she's in there somewhere
and she's in there praying for me.
Tell her it's safe to come home now.
There are two things she needs to see.
And tell her there's no need to worry.
You've done a good job on me.

Part One

Her Family

At first the life was loving,
but the love was just a lie.
Love's laughter is far behind us.
All hope has long since died.

And she brings with her the sadness
of a family in senseless shame.
They love to wallow in the mire.
Their souls are too numb to blame.

She drags around those memories,
too grotesque to have ever been known.
She heaves them on her shoulder.
That's not where they belong.

Their faces will soon disappear
and it won't take too long.
My children will not be theirs to mold.
They will never learn their song.

As for the girl, I know that she is safe.
And we all know what went wrong.
And I'll be the silent hero
though all the poetry is gone.

Locked In

The Grandmother

Repressed hatred is seeping through
for what The Grandmother did to you.
How could she simply decide
to lay her baby by his side?
She shows no guilt, no shame, no remorse.
Only regretting that you found your voice.

She has a sickening point of view.
She had two daughters from
which he could chose.
You were her little baby girl,
but she gave him your body to explore.
She offered you as a sacrifice,
such a small price to become his wife.

She wanted him so badly
and loves his memory to this day.
You were just a casualty,
a mere hurdle in the race.

Without an apology,
without a tear in her eyes,
she says she'd do it all again
and that GOD is on her side.

Facts are flying at me,
revealing more of her disgrace.
Someone needs to smack that smirk
right off her filthy face.
Reality is sinking in and
I'm finally seeing red.

The sun will shine a little brighter
once that wicked witch is…

Part One

Queen Evil

Queen Evil
seems to have a power
to confuse minds
and entrap them with her lure.
Abusers seem to get the sympathy.
Their victims left to find a cure.
On-lookers watch in silence.
The witnesses have lost their tongue.
The innocent becomes the liar.
So the alternates had to come.

Locked In

Still

The bottomless darkness
of your spirit,
still haunts me from within.
Still holds me captive,
sears me just beneath the skin.
You pummeled my body,
led it like a slave
and still,
you smile at the night
that my spirit finally gave.

Part One

Seeds

I ate from the tree of your
loathing for me.
I swallowed the juice
and digested all the seeds.

Locked In

Moods

I heard your scream.
A blood-curdling scream,
that sliced through layers of my sanity.
It pierced my eardrums,
making my feet run,
but in slow motion like in a bad dream.

Mommy is on the floor.
Kicking, screaming,
with eyes clenched and
pounding fists, jerking
in a violent, raging, tantrum?
Where is my mother,
the rock; my spiritual head?
And who is this screaming, "Chop, chop!"
and sending me under the bed
to be the smallest little girl no one could see?
Until I'd hear your laughter calling me.
To safety.

With that laughter, I knew I could breathe.
I could find recognition in those eyes.
For just a brief moment to treasure
because soon it would be time to hide.

Hide from the resentment and contempt,
bewildered anger and surprise,
lurking just behind your ebony eyes.
Surprise that I am here.
Surprised that I am.

Part One

But the change was so quick,
it would make my head spin.
In another moment you'd be gone again;
a day, maybe two,
but you always came back
with tons of presents in boxes and sacks.
All for the best little girl the world ever knew.

What I always thought were moods,
were really many different yous.

Locked In

Lost Mind
age 14

Pulling my hair.
Biting my nails.
Banging my head against the wall.
I'm losing my mind.
Trying not to hurt you.
Trying not to hate you.
I'm losing my mind.
The pacing back and forth.
The contemplation of suicide.
The crying out loud.
I'm losing…

Part One

Night Terrors

Cruel
haunting
sadistic
demon
prowlers.

Torturing
souls
long
since
devoured.

Locked In

The Girl in My Mind
age 14

There's someone in the corner of my brain
and I wish that she were me.
I think she was put there purposely
to stomp out my mind.
She's screaming out loud, begging for help.
There's no one to calm her down,
no one to help her get out.
She's trapped in this body that has no heart,
in a pool of unshed tears.
I think she's been growing there
for quite a number of years.
But she's quickly losing her patience.
Growing more and more indignant.
She's running and running
and jumping up and down.
She's building up her strength.
Gaining control.
One dark day she'll break on through,
and that will be the end of both of us.

Part One

Winter Kills
age 16

To be likened to a leaf,
could lead to fear and grief.
Leaves that start to fall,
full of everything but inner peace.
Turning from vibrant green to lifeless brown.
Falling steadily to the ground.
Being caught in nature's tug-of-war.
Pushed away by the cool wind,
then called back for more.
When the leaves are steadily falling,
their colors bent on turning,
they know their end is coming.
For winter kills.

Locked In

Cocaine
age 16

Dancing on the high wire
   to amaze the crowd below.
But you had no interest
   in my death defying show.

Part One

The Law Is Divine

Lying still, safely undercover.
Hiding from the eyes of the temple
she's smothered.
Dead, yet living the truth before brothers.
Her light tripped over the line.
HE locked the door behind.
Darkness had to fall,
for the law is divine.
When night has come,
and day is gone with the sun,
the corpse will rise and breathlessly run,
trying to return to the living; the light.
The heavens are still shining bright.
She had washed her robes
and made them white.
But she will die again this night

for the dead are too weak to fight.

She won't rise over and over, my friend,
trying to twist herself clean before men.
She'll be killed no more.
For she will never live again.

Locked In

Cry

Angry
words
stream
from
fingertips
staining
paper
with
words
that
never
dry
like
tears
would
stain
my
face
if
only
I
could
cry.

Part One

Spanking

Salty
pools of blood streaming from my lips.

Blind
and dazed; eyes still swollen shut.

Quiet panting
let's me know that you're still near.

Stench
the reeking, squalid, evil of you
permeates the room and mutilates my core.

Cold and Naked
weakened by your whip
arms and neck; blackened and blue
like my spirit.

Locked In

Tick
age 15

Somewhere between living and dying,
choked on silence, no tears left for crying.
Strangled by the grip of sin that's surviving.

You can run, but not outrun the fire.
Repentance was there, but retribution much higher.

Your days will begin and end this way.
Your love has grown cold
and dies more everyday.
You try to be strong,
pretend you're content.
Your heart has been bleeding.

Like a bomb, you begin to tick.

You could escape;
abandon all that you know.
But you'll go on smiling,
giving them a good show.
This is yours alone to suffer;
no one else has to know,
until the clock has stopped ticking
and this bomb explodes.

Part One

Daddy

I laid, waiting for deliverance,
watching you
hungrily watching me.
Your mouth foaming
as they inflicted
many types of pain on me.
Every thrust and
BRUTAL BITE
ignited your twisted appetite.
Your eyes glazed over,
amused at the sight.
With every second
your eyes grew more
EVIL and INTRIGUED.
Through each penetrating stab
your eyes remained firmly fixed on me.
You should have been my savior
but made no attempt to save me.
So, for you, I offer no forgiveness,
only this silent rage that has burned a
GAPING hole in me.
I can give it to you now,
because I am finally free.
And guess what DADDY,
your baby's got a gift to write.
Now everyone who reads will see
that you are
ONLY wicked,
and that's all you'll ever be.

Locked In

Images

I see myself through a vaporous haze.
I am never quite certain of what I see.
Like a bat out of hell, the image has changed.
A specter, which frightens the heck out of me!
These indistinct messages,
strangely deranged,
they batter my psyche
and damage my brain.
So I ask you plainly
to tell me the truth
and settle the quandary
that's plagued me from youth.

Do I frighten the wits out of children at play?
Do innocent babies recoil in dismay?
Do strangers who pass camouflage their surprise?
Are they smiling politely, while shunning my eyes?

Did nature construct me with mischief in view?
Was I spooned from the kettle of foul witches' brew?
Do my eyes deceive me like treacherous dreams?
I'm praying that it's not as bad as it seems.

Part One

Mirror, Mirror

I stare into a looking glass,
a golden mirror on the wall.
A wide-eyed girl looks back at me;
it seems she too, is mystified.

She's trying to communicate.
Her words?
The teardrops in her eyes.
It's strange, her tears disgrace my cheeks
and I can feel it when she cries.

This wide-eyed youngster saddens me.
She seems confused and unaware.
I don't know how to comfort her
so I just leave her standing there.

Locked In

Crazy Black Curls

Daddy's having a little girl.
I'm sure she'll be cute as can be
with dimpled cheeks and crazy black curls.

I hope she'll be your heart,
and that she'll always know.
I'm sure she'll giggle,
and you'll beam
when she dances on your toes.

I hope you hold her real tight.
Kiss away the fears she collects each night.
Tell her you'll slay all the dragons in her way.
Tell her about the secret places you visit everyday.

Cause little girls, they get scared and confused,
when first the monsters come into view;
to betray and seduce; monsters that look like you.
With eyes full of lewd intent,
they batter and bruise.
But little girls, they stay confused
and they'll struggle and fight,
for the rest of their lives,
making light of their plight,
trying to make you see that

she's just your little girl.
Worthy of being your little girl.
As cute as can be with crazy black curls.
Not alone in this cold, empty world.

Part One

Father
age 15

Seldom is a man left alone to cry.
Bothered by many.
Just left to die.
Told to leave,
doesn't go.
You hold out your hands.
He shakes his head no.
Looking right through you,
yet not seeing.
A man abusive,
cruel and taunting,
because he doesn't know the meaning of love.
That's what a father means to me.

Locked In

His Rational

It isn't my fault.
How could it be?
I gave you my all.
Why couldn't you see?

As for my secret life,
that was not your concern.
How could you be hurt?
Why did you discern?
I was careful to hide
my discretions from view.
You chose to perceive
so the fault lies with you.

No, I wasn't there,
but my presence was strong.
So, how can you judge that my
lifestyle was wrong.
You can only suspect.
Where is your proof?
I will not take the blame.
I diminish the truth.

And I will not recall
these abuses you claim.
You cannot make me see
and I will not explain.
I am spotless and clean
and my conscience is clear.
Your pain is your own.
There is no penance here.

Part One

Separation

Wandering aimlessly through the densest fog
is the empty separation from

GOD.

Locked In

Father's Reward

Who loves the light
and speaks the lie?
Full of dishonesty,
full of pride.
Haunted by a love
that led to deception.
Love's desire brought forth sin's erection.
Mental masturbation prolongs,
but lends no protection.
Does it lead to repenting's conception?
The heart of the sheep that holds the truth,
does it bleed true the color it was given
or shaded,
darkened by the secrets hidden?
Hidden from all those chosen to see,
but not from HIM who can see
and does see.
Oh, what a disappointment dedication can be.
Will you let it kill you during your birth?
You must be child
for on milk you still nurse.
And as for THE life,
YOU will never come to know,
for the promise is strong,
but the faith has to grow.
Protected and insane, trapped and deranged.
Dancing to the song Satan's angels sang.
And it is you,
it's been you all along.
Bringing them to mercy,
singing that sad song.

Part One

Because they know in their hearts
that you have deceived.
And with no proof they still believe.
HE gave them the knowledge,
the truth and the wisdom.
And with your lips
you've locked up the kingdom.
And the pain is great,
but the shame is much larger.
Their eyes have a stinging,
but their GOD has the power.
Over you.
To break you.
And you are reaping your reward in full.

Locked In

Locked In
age 14

Dear Lord, I killed my father today.
He was persistently cruel.
There was no other way.

He reminded me of my faults over and over again.
I was bound, within his sight, always locked in.
He loved to make me strip
then beat me until I could no longer feel.
He perfected his talent for torture on me.
So, his secrets I carefully concealed.

But those sleeping memories that haunt me
and awaken me each day,
mock me with a fear of remembering
and they quietly whisper his name.

Love will one day come for me,
I will look the other way.
Cause "I love you", means I'll hurt you
and I'm uneasy with such games.

I know that I should be sorry,
get down on my knees and repent.
I only wanted freedom.
Escape, my one intent.
I know in my heart,
I'd do it again.
And so, in jail I sit,
in so many ways,
locked in.

Part One

A Prayer for Forgiveness

I've known your wisdom.
In you I've found home.
I've felt your mercies
and blessings have been shown.
We all sing your praises.
But I sing alone.
How I ask for your forgiveness.
Show me the way home.
Please pour out your mercy
and wash my robes clean.
I know of your power.
I know of your love.
Please give me the strength,
holy spirit from above.
If only I could change what I've come to be.
Show me the way; I'm ready to leave.
I'm in love with your laws,
and the protection they breathe.
I beg your forgiveness,
and discipline I humbly receive.

Locked In

Praise

Marvel at the earth that GOD has created.
No one to talk to but I'm feeling elated.
The wind that is dancing,
it moves all around.
Caressing my face
yet it makes no sound.
The far away birds
sing of HIS praises.
Black and white children
search for new hiding places.
I'm amazed at the sun
shooting its blazes.
Leaving its mark
but on much darker faces.
It's a testimony!
How grand this place is.
How privileged we are
to witness HIS graces.
Praise HIM.
HE is deserving of our praise.

Part One

Cold Drink

You're like the coldest drink of water
on the hottest summer day.

Well, I drink and I drink
until my eyelids are full.

Somehow, I never feel refreshed.

Locked In

Hope
age 14

I've given up hope and I'm so confused.
This life's a mystery, with no break and no clues.
Hope is the key, without it we're lost.
Hope brings escape without any cost.
Hope is the thing that's kept me from falling.
I try to hang on but the pain, it keeps growing.
I hope for a time when I won't have to cry.
And people will know and not need to ask why.
Could it be true that the darkness will pass?
That my hopes, prayers and dreams
could come true at last?

Part One

Waste of Time

I never loved you; never cared.
I told you from the start,
'til time diverts eternity
no man would hold my heart.

I tried to block your path to me.
My walls were made of stone.
But you had plots
and points to prove;
agendas of your own.
You, determined in your heart
you would not be denied.
You showered me with bright bouquets,
stood staunchly by my side.

Then when you thought
you held the key and
finally had my heart,
you quickly bared your pointy teeth
to tear my flesh apart.

But I don't love you.
Never did.
I warned you from the start.
So your deceit and treachery
could never touch my heart.

Locked In

Shut Up

Sometimes, I just shake it off,
consider the source and let it slide.
Sometimes, though, I've had enough.
I just want to see your tongue-tied.

Part One

Nobody Knows, One

Nobody knows you better than me.
I know Dr. Jeckle.
I've seen Mr. Hyde.
Nobody knows any better than me.
You are death and decay inside.

Nobody Knows, Two

Nobody knows
the trouble I see.
Nobody knows,
not even me.

Locked In

Dead Men Tell No Tales

Never leave a heart alive.
Pierce it to make sure it's dead.
Never leave a soul intact.
Pound it 'til its blood is shed.
Never leave a mind in peace.
Bludgeon it until it wails.
Leave no tongue to testify.
Dead men tell no tales.

Part One

White Washed Grave

Just as I thought
you proved to be
the white washed grave
of misery.

Just as I thought
your sun-dried bones
pried open the crypt
and called it home.

Locked In

Destiny

I have walked one thousand miles.
I've crossed the raging sea.
I've endured torrential rains
to change my destiny.

I will leave the pain behind.
I laugh at treachery.
I will save my little boys
and change their destiny.

I will consecrate my space.
I'll learn sagacity.
I will soar to heavens' heights
to change my destiny.

Part One

Moving On

You brought me joy once, a long time ago.
But along the way I lost interest.
I learned more than you wanted to know.
Time graciously opened my eyes and
then showed me which way to go.
Now my days are filled with living
and my soul is without any holes.
I bring myself the joy now
in a happy ending that I so bravely chose.

Locked In

Marriott Midnights

11:55 p.m.
Another melted Saturday night.
While I sprint though the house
performing my nightly ritual,
I think of you, stretched out before your 61' inch TV
burping
and rubbing your fat and happy stomach.
I,
check the stove, trip over crayons,
fly up the steps three at a time,
wonder if I turned the curling iron off
and if you'll send another child support check
this century.
I kiss the boys still pressed together in my bed.
Steal another moment
to marvel at their beauty.
I slide down the stairs two at a time and
click off all the lights.
I dash to the front door telling myself,
"I'll only be five minutes late."
I open the door and
the silence of my neighbors' sleeping falls into me
and props itself up against my chest.
She whispers contented snores into my left ear
and intoxicates me with the saliva
running down her right cheek.
The icy knob nibbles at my fingers
as my watch eats into my wrist
like Satan knawing on a chicken bone.
An exhaustion wells up from the deepest part of me.

Part One

It races up my throat, making my lips quiver.
It gushes out my eyes, scorching my face
in its haste to reach the tip of my chin.
I drift to the phone to make the call
I've longed to make for 97 nights.

Back in my bed, nestled between the boys,
I know everything will be okay.
We will somehow eat.
And I will somehow buy shoes
for those Flintstone feet
with the perfect icicle toes
resting against my thighs.

And we will make do without you
or another midnight at the Marriott.

Locked In

The Greatest Gift

She could have been famous,
picked any field.
And she still could
if she had the will.

She'll sing you a song and
can shatter glass.
Put on anything at all
and wear it with class.

She's got it going on and you can tell.
An exotic beauty, brilliant mind as well.
This diva's a mystery, but here's one clue:
There's no limit to what she can do.

She could have been anything.
But was everything, too.
An underserved gift that nature can bring.
A delicate flower with a wedding ring.
A gift greater than any other.
Wrapped in bows, ribbons and lots of pretty strings.
What a wonderful package for a mother.

Part One

Truce

Where do we go from here
when it is what it is
and it was what it was
and I've said all I needed to say?

I do feel for the broken man you've come to be.
I do hear you when you call.
I do see you with your arms stretched out
and your head hangin' low.
Too old and weak to dodge the
multi-syllabic missiles I threw at you.

I know you're old and tired.
Well, I'm tired, too.
Too old and tired to spend my days hating you.
Yeah, I'm old and tired and I'm thu.

It was what it was
and what will be will be.

Locked In, Part Two
by Barbara Randall

Locked In, Two
The Preface

I've spent my life in pursuit of love and acceptance. The fear that someone, anyone, might dislike me is a weight that I've carried since childhood. This consuming desire, the very idea that everyone should like me, is irrational. I know now that such a goal is unattainable, for when you're true to yourself, respect yourself and you value yourself, you will tend to step on an occasional toe. Though my intellect embraces this reality, emotion is hard to subdue and so at times, I find that the unreasonable quest for affection, affection at any cost, continues. I know that this is a weakness of character. It's a quality that shames me.

I reveal this emotional defect to explain the dilemma I've faced in writing this book. A horrible truth needs to be told, not for my sake alone, but also for the benefit of so many others who have walked, are now walking, or who may someday walk in my shoes.

For the longest time, I walked alone, shackled and silenced by guilt and shame, carrying this burden, while pretending it didn't exist and inwardly reproaching myself for the pain I felt. I became aware of other tortured souls who suffered in silence, while a critical and uninformed world branded them with stigma. I considered the emotional cost; cost to myself and also to my loved ones. I determined that I was obligated to write this book.

Part Two

I am truly beyond the malice that had begun to blister and swell inside me. I was gagging, to the point of suffocation and chocking on words that were trapped in my throat. Disgorging this river of pent up emotion is helping me to heal, to understand and also, to forgive.

Mama, please believe that I will always love you, no matter what, but I pray that someday you'll find the strength to acknowledge my pain and I hope to someday hear the words, "I'm sorry."

— *Barbara Randall*

Locked In

Have You Seen My Little Girl?

Have you seen my little girl?
She's wandered off into the world.
I tried to keep her close to me.
Somehow she managed to break free.
She's much too young to be alone.
She'll be afraid so far from home.
No one will hear her when she cries.
No one will sing her lullabies.
This world is such a daunting place.
The wind will be against her face.
And pretty dreams and tidy plans,
will turn to ashes in her hands.

Have you seen my little girl?
She's wandered off into the world.
She visualized a new domain,
with azure skies and fields of grain.
But in the midst of pastures green,
lay hidden traps and snares unseen.
And clever lies and misery,
are doses of reality.
For fairy tales, the books she'd read,
had glamorized the road ahead.
I pray for her as night descends,
that she'll retrace her steps again.

Part Two

Men Deceive

I was fifteen and very naïve.
I didn't know how men deceive.
He wanted me to lay with him.
To show how much I cared for him.
He needed me to prove my love
by giving him my everything.

I wanted him to hold me near.
To feel his warmth against my ear.
I only needed gentle words,
holding hands, a gentle touch.
I needed him to honor me,
to treasure and revere my trust.

And so, he promised
he would wait
although, his need for me was great.
If only he could 'touch' me there.
Caress my body everywhere.

Just enough to ease the pain
that young men feel when they abstain.
He'd force himself to be content.
He wouldn't use his instrument.

I didn't know what we had done
until a life began to form.
I was fifteen and so naïve;
how could I know that men deceive?

Locked In

Erika
age 16

The angels smiled in heaven,
and Gabriel blew his horn.
The earth stood still expectantly
when Erika was born.

A tiny spark of happiness,
a life so fresh and new.
She came to make my world complete
and make my dreams come true.

The Bible says no one will face
more pain than he can bear.
It says, for every quandary,
a blessing will appear.
When God sent me this precious gift
of love beyond compare,
it fortified my strong belief
in what is written there.

Part Two

Hope, II

For as long as you breathe,
for as long as you live,
you have purpose in life,
you have something to give.
Be it simply a smile, or a listening ear,
you are vital, somehow, there's a reason you're here.
When you're feeling the test and can't muster a smile,
when you walk in the rain and each inch is a mile,
when you've shaken the hand of the dismal abyss,
and intoxicate death with a sensuous kiss,
when you finally attain to the height of despair,
and the scorch of the sun burns your flesh everywhere,
and you measure your worth as a speck in the scale,
and your curse is to strive and your fate is to fail,
for you squander and waste and have nothing to share,
so you know you should die
and the world wouldn't care.
When you truly believe there's no basis for hope,
and credulity reigns as the costliest joke,
when your life is a maze,
and you haven't a clue,
and there is no reprieve, in whatever you do,
and the pain is too great and you long to be free,
and the holocaust thrives and it's all you can see,
don't give up in the fight.
Share your burden with me.
I'm your reason to live.
I'm your reason to be.

Locked In

Nature's Spotlight

I have always felt your pain.
And shared that fear you couldn't name.
I analyzed your sad refrain.
Your musings broke my heart.
I cried for you when you were low.
I prayed for strength to help you grow.
And silent screams were meant to show,
I loved you from the start.
But muted words, though they be true,
invoke no brilliance, tone or hue,
like fields of green or skies of blue,
and other works of art.

See, I was trained to hibernate,
safe inside my slumber state.
So how could I participate
or join you in the fray?

Then I perceived the day star rise,
when intellect unveiled my eyes.
I saw my role in your demise.
My penance is dismay.

I stand here now, beyond the gate,
desperate to clear the slate,
seeking ways to compensate
as mother and as friend.

Part Two

Cognizance has trickled in.
I can see your eyes again.
Eyes that blaze a fiery hue.
Eyes that scream, "I'm watching you."
Eyes accusing, eyes that tell.
Eyes that viewed a man made hell.

Eyes that boast resiliency.
I'm proud of what you've come to be.

No need to apologize for the anger in your eyes.
What you've lived has made you wise.

Now claim your mark and take your cue.
Nature's spotlight shines on you.

Locked In

Retrospect

I wish I had known.
I wish I had seen.
Your colors were gray.
I saw vibrant green.
Your heart was a gift
that you held in your hands.
You screamed out to me with your silent demands.
My eyes were wide shut.
My senses were bound.
I heard your distress,
but I muted the sound.
You needed my strength to comfort your soul,
but my mind was a mess,
spinning out of control.
Still, you were supreme
and your hurt was my own.
So I die in the thought,
that I left you alone

Part Two

Tisha

Do you know how grand you are?
Do you see what others do?
Do you see the treasures rare
deep within the heart of you?

You are more than silken skin.
More than just a pretty smile.
I scrutinize the depths of you
and know my life has been worthwhile.

Peer inward thru those dazzling eyes.
Past that perfect angel face.
Deeper than those dimpled cheeks.
Peer into your sacred place.

Deep within the soul of you
where true beauty does not fade.
Peer into your secret place.
See the gift that Jah has made.

Locked In

Impotence

I know it's been the longest time,
It's hard to sort things out.
One moment brings such clarity,
the next engenders doubt.

While searching for the bluest sky
I'm wilting in the rain,
where passion is absurdity
and fervor summons pain.

I've tried to cross that boundary
where greener pastures grow.
To visualize that wonderland
where healing waters flow.

But mortal man cannot presume
to rescind history.
And so my fettered soul concedes
to never be set free.

Part Two

The Five-Second Rule

His hourglass knows,
the firm grip of his hand.
Its sands start to flow,
when you look at a man.
The message is clear
and its vengeance is cruel.
There's no escaping,
this merciless tool.
There's never a reason,
for more than a glance.
If you offer a smile,
then you're taking a chance.
Pay any attention,
the risk is your own.
The fist in your face,
will be your fault alone.
There can be no occasion,
and no circumstance
that gives you permission,
to laugh or to dance.
This regulation is etched in stone.
It pricks the marrow,
and pierces the bone.
This five-second rule will always apply.
When you're knocked to the ground,
you don't need to ask why.

Locked In

Laugh

You just gotta laugh.
What else can you do?
He boggles the brain
but he tickles it, too.

Part Two

The Tyrant

The tyrannical beast is losing his power.
Omnipotence dies.
Reticence thrives.
I scrutinize the cowardly eyes of the bully.

Locked In

Fantasy

"I'm the hope you contemplate,
here to pluck you from the sea.
I'll purge the water from your lungs.
Breath of life abides in me."

Reality

The man I married proved to be,
the blow that knocked the life from me.

Part Two

Insanity

You teetered for the longest time.
Then languidly, you crossed the line.
With one small step you ventured in.
And now you can't cross back again.

Locked In

Compromise

She loved him so.
The bonds were strong.
With velvet voice
he sang a song.
He learned his prey.
Inflamed her need.
With bogus charm
he masked his greed.
And when she knew,
she compromised.
Refused to hear her babies' cries.
Afraid to fight…she never tried.
What could she do?
Her hands were tied.

Part Two

Exasperation

I really feel the need to curse.
I think that GOD would understand.
If I hold it in, I know, I'll burst.
Lord, I've had it with that man.

Locked In

Incest
by an unnamed alternate personality

I never saw his face.
Don't recall when he was born.
Was he once a child?
No, from Hades he was torn.
He always seemed mature,
but his victim was a child.
He kept venom in his teeth,
but they dazzled when he smiled.

His omnipotence was felt
in the marrow of my soul.
His energy abounds.
He never grows old.
I was sure I'd seen his strength;
the apex of his power.
So, I nullified the fear.
How could he hurt me more?

We made a bitter pact.
He would torment me alone.
I'd silently submit.
He'd possess the throne.
I honored his requests.
I bowed to each demand.
We sealed the horrid deal.
I took his slimy hand.

My babies would be safe.
He molested me at will.

Part Two

At some point in time,
he reneged on the deal.
He slithered from my bed,
put his filthy hands on you.

I didn't realize,
until you told me it was true.
He had looked me in the face,
and ruthlessly, he lied.
Now, I was in a place,
where the truth couldn't hide.
Now, I embrace emotions
that I never knew I had.
This isn't merely hurt,
I'm stark raving mad!

Locked In

Pandora's Box

I'm afraid of the dark.
I'm afraid of the light.
I'm afraid to let go
or to hold on too tight.

I am frightened to speak
but, then silence is cold
and my soul is ablaze
with the secrets I hold.

The truth makes me bleed.
The lie is a ghost
and I can't be sure
which will haunt me the most.

I've taken the key
from Pandora's hand.
The shadow she cast
is where I now stand.

This is an alternate ending to Pandora's Box
by an unnamed alternate personality

I kneel before Pandora's box
I reach for it with trembling hand
I know the anguish she unleashed.
In her shadow I now stand.

Part Two

Casualties of War
Part 1, Casualty of War

My son is wounded to the core,
a patent casualty of war.
His flesh is torn. His faith is numbed.
His fate was sealed when I succumbed.
He's not to blame; the cards were dealt
with no regard for what was felt.
And on his tomb, in effigy,
I carve the words, "a travesty".
For all my love has failed to save
this precious life my carcass gave.

Part 2, Legacy

My little girl enchants the eye.
She smiles the smile and lives the lie.
And pain that throbs so deep within,
has yet to mar her pretty skin.
I think it's better that we scream
and vocalize the frights we've seen.
For wounds that fester cannot mend;
they bleed and breed and rise again.
And each new life we come to share
will join us in the pain we bear.
And generations carry on
this legacy we pass along.
This legacy took root in me
and blossomed unabashedly.
And with regret, I passed it on
to dimpled cheeks and eyes that shone.

Locked In

Part 3, Her Way

I know a little girl
who is very much like me.
She's fragile, yet she's strong.
And though she is naïve
she's also wise beyond her years.

In furtive desperation
her laughter veils dismay,
and simulated smiles
have camouflaged her pain.
She is greatly prized
and feels the warmth of love.
But when shadows come to slay the sun
she's left baffled and bemused.
She sees the paradox:
just beyond her reach
lies the Promised Land.

Her sharp eyes gauge the distance.
Her heart tucks hope away.
A fertile mind gives birth
to amazing fabrication.
She lays claim to a world…
a world of her own making.
A fantasy conceived and
born in frustration.

Darkness can't prevail here.
For how can doom descend
where daylight never ends?

Part Two

This land of incantation
was established on pretense.
The child composed the script
and she directs the play.
She amends the words
and decides which scenes should stay.
She turns emotion inward.
She hasn't much to say.
This is her salvation.
This becomes her way.

Locked In

Vexation

I try to understand.
I do want to help.
I never throw you scraps.
I've sacrificed my needs and
I give until it hurts.
I'm the one you call
when no one else will come.
But when I reach my hand to you
with food for your soul
with no motive other than a wish
to see you whole,
you bite the hand that feeds you.

Part Two

Despicable Sin

When he would sob
and great tears would flow,
his heart wrenching words
would torture my soul.
He promised to never destroy me again
and to clothe me forever in love without end.

He swore on his life
and on heaven above
to slave for my heart and treasure my love.

He had studied his prey
and grown cunning and wise.
So he knew what to say
to secure my demise.
Like malleable clay,
he molded my mind
'til logical doubt became harder to find.

He molded my mind
to forgive him again
and to blindly repeat my despicable sin.

Locked In

Locked In, II
by Bobbie

Dear Lord, she killed her dad today.
She knew it was the only way.
He filled her cup with misery,
and sabotaged her sanity.
His machinations found their mark,
when schemes were plotted in the dark.
Yet even in the light of day,
the terrors didn't go away.
The desperation grew extreme,
'til haunted eyes began to stream.
And tears that fell like April rain,
found solace in the thoughts that came.
Thoughts that blossomed in her brain,
rooted in the fertile pain.
Now her heart was pacified.
Hope was born and tears were dried.
And though she knew that it was wrong,
it wasn't for herself alone.
She was forced to do the deed,
so other hearts would cease to bleed.
She did it for the tears I cried,
for years of hurt I kept inside.
She did it to erase the pain,
and end the tyrant's evil reign.
Her brother and her sister too,
lived in his perverted zoo.
Neither was as old as she.
Someone had to set them free.
Now they're locking her away.

Part Two

Much too high a price to pay.
Please God make them understand,
why she had to kill that man.
Help her to articulate,
that he taught her soul to hate.

Please God help them all to see,
she learned violence at his knee.
And when she came across his gun,
she did just what I should have done.
The thought keeps pulsing in my head:
It should have been my act, instead.
And so, when they asked me why
I just sat and watched him die,
what other answer could I give?
He simply had no right to live!

Locked In

Questions

What drives that man?
What makes him tick?
Is he mean,
or is he sick?

Part Two

My Wish

If I was granted just one wish,
and what I wished would come to be,
I'd travel to a happy place,
and take my babies there with me.

Locked In

Shackles

For one fleeting moment,
I plotted escape.
I would gather my children and alter their fate.
I would gently arouse them,
flee into the night.
We'd awaken to blue skies,
to sunshine and light.

But one fleeting moment
of rhythm and rhyme
is here and then gone.
A mere fraction of time.
And fear is revived
in one beat of the heart.
And so, fate, yet again, is a pit in the dark
where malevolent forces
command me to see
that my innocent babies
are shackled to me.

Part Two

Sinking

Bottomless pit
Abysmal descent
Squandering time
Fruitless intent
Enamored with death
Embracing the tomb
Relinquishing hope
To savor the gloom
Pavlovian tears
Drench weary eyes
Irrational fears
Envision demise

Locked In

Dreams

I thought of you the other day.
I dreamed of you that night.
Awake or sleep, you trouble me.
Now, you know that ain't right!

Part Two

Hissy Fit

Guess I had a hissy fit.
Guess I had a right.
Threw his woman in my face.
Made me wanna fight.

Locked In

Inside Suicide
by Aurelia Curry

I heard voices.
They made me mad.
Not angry that they were speaking;
but upset that I could hear them.
The voices were kind and soothing,
and I knew that they wanted to help.
None of this was their fault.
I had botched it.
Again.
There would be repercussions.
Consequences I couldn't face.

I asked those voices if I would die.
Desperation razored my voice.

A pretty blond woman was holding my hand.
She squeezed it and assured me that I would not die.

She had misunderstood!

Her eyes cast shadows of shrouded concern.
My own sadness was mirrored there.

But why?
What could she know and why should she care?

Part Two

It was all so confusing.
My head ached.
Acerbic bile assaulted my throat.
Guilt became a ravenous wolf.
It wasted no time.
It gobbled me up!

I would ignore the throbbing pain
because I had done this to myself.
I deserved the pain.

I asked again, "Are you sure I won't die?"
There were tears in my eyes
and my voice was a prayer.
I was praying real hard,
for the possibility.
For just a little hope.

The sad blond woman was stroking my hair.
She leaned close to whisper,
"You're going to be fine.
You're not going to die.
I turned from her,
and sank into my pillow.
Soon, it was wet, like the hair on my brow.

She had misunderstood!

I had failed again,
and so I would live.
We all would.
And our circumstances were no better.

Maybe worse.

Locked In

Depression

I closed my eyes and filled my brain
with nothingness to dull the pain.

Part Two

Mitigation
by Elizabeth

We saw what she intended to do.
She tried to hide it,
but we knew.

Some of the others egged her on.
We tried to stop them
but they were too strong.

I don't blame her.
Her intentions were good.
She did it because she believed she should.

She was trying to do us a favor that day.
Besides, sometimes
you just feel that way.

Locked In

Our Poem
by The Babies

The medicine made us sick so we cried.
We don't know who took the medicine.
We woke up with a tummy ache.
We didn't know anybody there.
They wouldn't let us go home to our mommy.
We wanted our mommy.

Part Two

Memories
by G.

I remember the ammonia.
I vaguely recall the bleach.
I remember the razors
and the hoarding of pills,
and the knives in the purse
for emergencies.
(An emergency was anytime she felt she had to do it!)

I remember the hunger,
when she wouldn't let us eat.
We were freakishly thin,
and looked older than our years.

We're still weak and we tire easily.
We never sleep and we're freezing
because there's no meat on our bones.
But she still says she's fat.

I'm the voice of reason.
Like a child, I tell her the same things
over and over again.
I'll preach the same sermon
'til I finally get through.

You never give up on someone you love.
And although she frustrates me,
I have always loved her.

Locked In

Island Girl

I'm looking for this woman
of the warm island sun.
I've only heard about her,
I'm not certain where she's from.
She sounds extraordinary,
uninhibited and free.
I find it quite intriguing,
that she lives inside of me.
They tell me she's exotic.
They say she has flair.
She tempers that flamboyance,
with a confidant air.
I want to know her deeply.
I want to know her name.
I wonder if she likes me.
I wonder why she came.
I feel sorry for her.
She's very far from home.
If I could get to know her,
she wouldn't be alone.
And one day,
when I'm stronger,
she'll be free to run
to the white-sand beaches,
of the warm island sun.

Part Two

Island Dream
by Bobbie

Let's lie in the grass and look at the sun,
and dream of the beaches where I used to run.
Where crystal blue waters are kissing the sand,
while I kiss the lips of an island man.

We'll gather the seashells that garnish the shore,
and all take an oath not to worry no more.
We'll each feel at peace,
as we walk hand in hand,
on a sandy white beach,
with a tall island man.

Locked In

No Vacancy

You have no idea.
How could you know?
We tend to dismiss
what's within our control.
How freely you move,
unencumbered through life.
Yet, you fall in the face
of miniscule strife.

But you can make plans
knowing you'll follow through.
Your mind is an ally,
it's working with you.
You know where you've been
and you know what you've done.
And the life that you lead
is a bask in the sun.

Does a taste, or a smell,
or a sound bring you pain?
Are you shackled to rituals
that you can not explain?
Do you face each new task
with the fear of defeat?
Does your stomach turn
when you know you must eat.
Are you scared of the dark
and of falling asleep?
Do you ever choke,
on the secrets you keep?

Part Two

Do you check and count to the point of despair?
Have you ever heard voices
when no one was there?
I'm sharing a body
that's run out of room.

There are too many tenants
with voices that boom.
So many fears and a need to confide,
but I'm so often hurt; it's much safer to hide.
There are taunts and derision
and minds that won't budge.
And hateful opinions
from strangers who judge.
But since you can't know
what a person's been through,
it's foolish to judge,
it could happen to you.

Locked In

Lessons
by Barbara 2

You've taught me much in these few years.
I've learned of pain and hurt and tears.
I've learned defeat and dark despair.
I've learned distrust and not to care.
I've learned that men with silken tones,
can freeze the heart and chill the bones.
That words are only hollow things.
And promises are empty dreams.
To keep myself from falling hard,
I've learned it's wise to stay on guard.
For men use games as hurtful tools.
They lie and cheat and change the rules.
But efforts to enslave my soul,
have missed their mark and failed their goal.
For evil schemes that haunt the night,
have been exposed in morning light.
I'm glad for this veracity,
because the truth does set you free.
And now that you have dropped the reign,
I'll learn to trust in love again.

Part Two

Multiples

The world is a stage.
I believe this is true.
We each have a role.
I stand at my mark
and I know my cue.

But too many voices direct me.
Too many hands
pushing and pulling,
issuing demands.
My vision fades.
Darkness descends.
I cross the thin line,
and intellect lingers behind.

The thing I fear most, grabs hold.
I accuse myself.
I excuse myself.
Now strangeness descends.
Voices assure me,
"We are trying to help."
The voices attack
and add to the terror.

Locked In

Alone in the Trenches
by The Newcomer

I can't say why I'm here.
It's so late in the game.
But I find myself here,
without even a name.

I fell into a trench
with a man I don't know.
I was sizing him up
when he landed a blow.

The specifics are blurred
and I don't want to fight.
And I feel so alone
with no counsel in sight.

The others are near,
but they only survey.
And the insight they hold
they refuse to convey.

It is mutual distrust
that keeps us apart,
but we'll need to unite
to master this art.

Part Two

Ignorance is Mean

You don't need to carry me.
You don't need to hold my hand.
I've survived a battlefield
and I know that I can stand.
You don't need to speak for me.
Listen to my steady voice.
My decisions honor me.
Time will validate my choice.
You don't need to pity me,
but I do deserve a chance.
Don't insult my dignity
with your hollow song and dance.
I'm the wounded of this world,
but my wounds can not be seen.
You're ignorant of this malady.
Your ignorance has made you mean.
So ask me how the brain can hurt
and ask me how the soul can bleed.
Then reassess the strengths in me.
Appearances mislead.

Locked In

Peter's Song
for Linda

She told me not to sing that song.
The song that Peter loved to play.
She told me to ignore the words,
and make the music go away.
She told me that I had a voice,
and music that the world should hear.
She said my music touched her heart,
and I should sing it loud and clear.

Linda said the words I wrote,
and my plaintive melodies,
were instruments to heal my hurt
and purge my insecurities.

But Peter didn't like my songs.
He said my words were shallow streams.
He said my music didn't flow,
that I was lost in futile dreams.
He told me that I needed him.
Without him I would fade away.
He'd ridicule each simple tune,
and hold my confidence at bay.

I breathed these evil taunts for years.
Inhaled his enigmatic lies.
The demon music that he made,
removed the vision from my eyes.

He labored on a toxic brew,
a potion to make friendships die.

Part Two

And when the venom kissed my lips,
she vanished with a tortured sigh.
Still, Linda's words were haunting me.
Calling out through time and space,
"You don't need to cling to him.
You deserve a better place."

Now the years have come and gone.
There is no more woman-child.
I have learned to chart my own course.
I have learned to love my style.

And I found my friend again.
I stand before her proud and strong.
Much more certain of my step,
and enamored with my song.

Sometimes, still, in quiet night,
Peter's music comes to call.
I recognize the daunting voice,
but I can't hear his words at all.
His melody is obsolete,
and his lyrics are all wrong.
I'm unfamiliar with the beat.
I've long forgotten Peter's song,
but Linda's words will echo on.

Locked In

Pain

You've had
your day
of vile increase.
Now, go away
I've earned my peace.

PART TWO

The Grass Is Always Greener

The more you sought
the less you found.
You turned your head
toward every sound.
You scoured the world
in search of gold
and bought each myth
that you were sold.

I'd mock you,
but it's just too sad.
You never knew
what wealth you had.
In afterthought,
I gotta say,
"I told you so!
Now, go away".

Locked In

Lime Green Dress

I married him in a lime green dress.
A real expensive lime green dress.

My hair was cut into a 'bob'.
Like Jackie O.,
I wore a bob.

I kind'a teetered down the aisle.
Teetered on my heels, too high.

Somebody made my face up.
I can't recall who made me up.

I cried off all my makeup.
I really ruined my makeup.

The tears,
they stained my pretty green dress.
Now whatever became of that lime green dress?

Part Two

Too Late

You tell me that you love me still.
And promise that you always will.
It saddens me that you don't see
your love delivered death to me.

You tell me that you cannot live
unless I promise to forgive.
It puzzles me that you don't know
your love became the fatal blow.

You tell me of your misery.
You need the love that used to be.
But love is such a fragile thing,
it withers without nurturing.

You're asking for an open door,
to claim the heart you held before.
But broken hearts turn into clay,
they turn to dust and blow away.

Locked In

Consequence

What goes around, comes around,
you don't worry me.

What goes around, comes around,
you'll share my agony.

What goes around, comes around,
you'll feel the wrath one day.

For every ounce of devilment
there is a price to pay.

Part Two

Funny

I didn't know your heart could feel
the emptiness, the icy chill,
the acid burn, the constant ache,
the sting that doesn't dissipate.

But now you say you deeply yearn
to make my heart your one concern.
It's funny how the tables turn.

It's funny how the tables turn!

Locked In

Fate

What if we hadn't met that day,
or I had turned and walked away.
What if I hadn't been naïve
and I had learned to disbelieve.
What if the baby hadn't come?
My pretty little precious one.
What if I'd chosen to refuse
to wed a man I didn't choose?
I could have vanished with my child
instead of walking down the aisle.
What if we'd never met that day,
or I had turned and walked away.

Part Two

There's A Baby On Your Hip
by Bobbie

There's a baby on your hip.
Be careful that she doesn't slip.
Funny how she dangles there,
 like a cuddly teddy bear.
How'd you learn this juggling act?
When'd you know you had the knack?
Sure does work out well for you.
Cause there's so much you have to do.
Laundry, dishes, cooking meals,
 telephoning, paying bills.
But she's at your fingertip,
 while she's safe upon your hip.
She's so happy riding there.
Perched upon her 'mommy chair'.
Pleasure dances in her eyes,
 like excited butterflies.
Mommies hip is sheer delight.
She's astride both day and night.
Much better than a pony ride.
How could she not be satisfied?
Chubby hands and dimpled feet,
 kick and flail a frantic beat.
Don't even try to put her down.
Her gleeful grin turns upside down.
Precious little baby thing,
 needs eternal nurturing.
So, I guess she'll have to stay,
 perched upon your hip that way.

Locked In

Ode To Alice
for my only sister, whom I truly love

As time went by, I wondered why I never got a line.
"But don't dismay" my heart would say,
"Be patient; give her time."
This busy life so full of strife,
can stifle our intent.
We mean to write but not tonight.
Thus there the moment went.
Though months went by,
I didn't cry.
I knew that soon there'd be,
a letter, sweet, in cursive, neat,
intended just for me.
So, I'll just wait,
a Godly trait,
and not feel out of joint.
Yet, still no word,
from you is heard,
which brings me to this point.
A nagging doubt came creeping out,
a doubt that turned to fear.
What if these months,
should all at once,
become a lunar year?
I think I'll write.
I'll write tonight.
I'll ask you, "what's the deal"?
I'll take time now,
someway, somehow.
I'll tell you how I feel.

Part Two

I miss you so,
you'll never know.
I wish that you were here.
You're smiling face,
and warm embrace,
can only bring me cheer.

And when you're low,
I need to know,
to tell you that I care.
There is no doubt,
I'd DIE without this friendship that we share.
So, drop a line, to say,
"I'm fine" and
send along a smile.
Though we're remote,
your blissful note will
cheer me for a while.

Locked In

When Butchie Died

I was there when Butchie died.
I felt the pain take root inside.
I absorbed the misery.
Bewilderment confounded me.
Hurtful words were sinking sand and
reasonings hard to understand,
sent me running from the light,
out of reach and out of sight.
Still, I cuddled with the guilt,
familiar as Big Mama's quilt.
I was pleased to slumber there.
Seemed as safe as anywhere.
Still, I wallow in the blame.
Harboring fears I cannot name.
Recently, I saw his face.
Smiling, in a happy place.
From an ancient photograph,
I could hear my brother's laugh.
Insight caused a bell to ring.
Genesis was beckoning.
Gentle eyes were trained on me,
eyes that spoke, consolingly.
I glimpsed the message written there.
Read the thoughts he sought to share.
For just one minute speck of time,
Butchie vaporized the crime.
Discomfiture was rooted out.
Confidence displaced the doubt.
Shame was banished from my heart.
Pubescent? Yes.
But still, a start!

Part Two

For The Pumpkins

Delinquent child.
Lousy wife.
Neglectful mom.
Cursing life.
Brought full circle.
Cycle ends
with the help of
little friends.
My own blood and my own flesh,
misery was laid to rest.
Precious love,
flows to me,
offered unconditionally.
Sugared words;
sweet commands,
I am putty in their hands.
No deficit; there's only gain;
silken bonds inflict no pain.

Locked In

Mama's Sisters

I can imagine you running through fields.
"Running wild", Big Mama would say.
I can imagine the chores you did,
up with Big Mama, at break of day.
Now, you're on the back of Big Daddy's old truck,
laughing and talking and loving the sun.
I love to imagine you safe in your beds,
happy when day is done.

Part Two

Tears

I held out
long as I could.
I begged and I pleaded,
and stated my case.
But none of that balling
did me no good;
just left me with tears on my face.

Locked In

For The Grandparents
*In memory of Emma "Big Mama"
and Luther "Big Daddy" Curry*

A little house, on a red dirt road,
sits stately and serene.
Its kingdom is the field that grows,
an endless sea of green.
I see it clearly, even now,
in scenes of yesterday,
the winding road to a country house,
where childhood memories stay.
I see the weathered pick-up truck,
parked over by a shed.
I see us riding in the back,
it's vivid in my head.
Big Daddy, in a cane-backed chair,
tipped up against a wall,
would sit out on the big front porch,
as night began to fall.
He whittled with a pocketknife,
we listened at his knee.
He told us tales of long ago,
from before we came to be.
And from inside the front screen door,
Big Mama hums a hymn.
She's working still at some odd task
as daylight starts to dim.
These people taught us simple things,
the lessons that endure.
They taught with warmth and strength,
and love to make the lessons sure.

Part Two

They planted seeds of love to grow,
for nurturing to start.
They painted pictures for the mind,
and values for the heart.
In vivid recollection,
still, it's firmly understood,
these simple, kind, hardworking folk,
inclined toward the good.
And smiles that twinkled in their eyes,
and somehow lingered there, gave just a glimpse,
of hearts alive, with love enough to share.
So now, when crickets lullaby,
and the moon begins to glow,
I watch the skies, contented,
as the stars put on their show.
I'm remembering another time.
I'm at Big Daddy's knee.
And I still hear the cadence
of Big Mamma's melody.
I still feel their goodness,
and the way they loved me so.
And I love them just as much
today, as I loved them long ago.

Locked In

A Little Girls Eyes

In a little girls eyes,
so large and round,
I see yesterday.
Saddened eyes,
cast a frown,
and then turn away.
Through these eyes, I recall,
what I felt when I was small.
In her eyes I can see,
she's standing now where I used to be.

I recall such misery,
and pain that no one else could see.

Because a land of make-believe,
shrewdly taught me to deceive.
And hurtful feelings of disgrace,
drove me to my secret place.
A magic place where solace grew,
and pleasures were abundant, too.
A place where I could be alone,
and each decision was my own.

But this land of sweet beguile,
could only soothe me for a while.
For when the real world filtered in,
I was knowing once again.
Then I'd bow my head to pray,
words my heart alone could say.
Begging GOD to intervene;
righting wrongs that thrived unseen.

Part Two

Praying, "Please GOD, let them know,
what I'm too afraid to show.

Let just one soul scrutinize,
the depths of these enormous eyes.
If someone would only ask,
I could toss away the mask."

Then vulgar secrets I concealed
could breach the wall and be revealed.
I feared that I had prayed in vain,
for my salvation never came.
But now, I know my thoughts were wrong,
for Jah is wise and very strong.
And earthly man can lose his sight,
in darkened skies or piercing light.
So, we can't see HIS master plan
or that he holds us in his hand.

But now a truth has crystallized,
within the strangely haunting eyes,
of a little girl that no one sees.
A child who hides her miseries.

In a magic land of her own design,
solace calms her fertile mind,
but only for a while…

Well, I can truly understand,
and I will always hold her hand.

Locked In

Her pain won't reign eternally.
Her magic land is here with me.
I'll break her chains and set her free,
and grant safe passage through the sea.
And when this journey finds its end,
she'll find her own two feet again.

I cling to her, religiously,
for who I was and who she'll be.
And when she masters self-belief,
she, too, will lift the torch.

And as for me, the pain I've known,
has nurtured fruitage I have grown.
For in the darkest circumstance,
I found a way to sing and dance.
The dancing vitalized my song.
The laughter kept me holding on.
Now, I'm obliged to share the wealth
to advocate a sense of self.
For when one heart is fortified,
it justifies each tear I cried.

I plot my course most cautiously,
for trusting eyes are trained on me.

We can't escape the road ahead.
This life is not a rose-clad bed.
But as we walk our brutish path,
I'll teach one sad-eyed child to laugh.

Part Two

A Soft Place To Fall
for Kathy

If we believe that we are loved,
and we feel our value and worth,
if we are taught and told,
but also, shown,
then we will be at peace
within a hostile land.

And when the thunder roars
and ill winds start to blow,
we slumber through the night,
sheltered from the storm.

And then we will abide,
like precious sheep of the fold.

And if we should stray,
when we hear the shepherd's call,
we will not be afraid.
We will fall into his arms.

A soft place to fall.

Locked In

Credulity

I tried to tell you long ago,
but you were disinclined to hear.
One cynic speaks a chilling word
and accolades all disappear.

The truth is naked to your eyes,
but you prefer the daunting fear.
You purse your lips to kiss the lie
and accolades all disappear.

It's wearisome to fight alone,
this skirmish is futility.
Your slumber started long ago,
now somnolence is calling me.

My efforts are a vanity.
My sentiments do not adhere.
You trust the crafty serpent's tongue
and accolades all disappear.

Part Two

Your Husband

The love of your life.
Your reason to be.
He was your prize.
It should have been me.

Locked In

Charlatan
by Barbara 2

It astonishes me,
the words you choose.
They shift the blame,
and then excuse.
And even when I'm sure you lie,
your words so easily pacify.

You have the strength to cause me pain.
Still, I excuse your words again.
You're speech so deftly searches out,
productive seeds that harvest doubt.

And like the tricky charlatan,
who leaves you, vaguely questioning,
you bid farewell, we part as friends
and then the cycle starts again.

Part Two

Wanton
by an unnamed alternate personality

You have no grace, no dignity.
You have no sense of style.
You wink your eyes and flash your teeth
in simulated smile.
You love the way the men react.
The way the fellas drool.
You crave the vulgar compliments;
pathetic little fool.
You miss the smirk behind their lips,
the sneer behind their eyes.
You strut your stuff
and swing your hips.
You better recognize!
Wanton women come and go
and never make a mark.
They blaze real hot
then fizzle out
and fade into the dark.
So you connived, deceived and lied
with profit as your aim.
You lay with him, in arrogance
upon a bed of shame.
You found what you most coveted,
to dominate his show.
I found the path from infancy
and so, began to grow.
So all you ever took from me
was hindrance and dismay.
So little girl, go check yourself
and run away and play.

Locked In

Think
by an unnamed alternate personality

She hit you with fists.
Stabbed you with words.
She beat you for things
she supposed you might do.
For the venting of anger,
or maybe just for fun.
She belittled your worth
and rejected your love.
Her apathy was more than a slap to the face,
worse than a blow to the head.
She stripped you naked.
She laid your soul bare.
A pitiful heap in the deepest despair.
She wouldn't believe what you needed to say.
She wouldn't protect you from harm in the way.
She left you alone in a turbulent sea.
What she didn't know was you always had me.
You dismiss every memory, to let the pain go.
But I have to ask what I most need to know.

Why must you persist in loving her so?

Part Two

Irony

One

It's been raining all day.
Thunderous clouds rule the sky.
All the world is a tomb.
And I just want to die.

Two

It's been sunny all day.
Not a cloud in the sky.
All the world is in bloom.
And I just want to die.

Locked In

Time

Where did my life go?
How can this be?
Time was a phantom
that I couldn't see.

I was only a baby
when time ran away.
It left in such haste
though I begged it to stay.

My vision has dimmed and my energy wanes.
My body's discovered my Big Mama's pains.
And the face in the mirror that gazes at me,
is my mother's face as it used to be.
When did my Nubian locks start to gray?
When did my features begin to decay?

Time, you're a thief
and you're robbing me blind!
You're just out of reach
in a place we can't find.
You're marching along
at an insolent pace.
I'm gauging your speed
by the lines on my face.

You think of yourself
as Conquering King.
And you smirk and you boast
that your reign is supreme.

Part Two

What you do not know
is that Jah has a will.
And once it's accomplished
you will stand still!

Locked In

Don't Ask

Don't ask me how I feel,
when tears begin to flow.
Don't ask if I'm alright.
You don't really want to know.

Don't flash your phony smile,
if your road should wind my way.
Don't let a question fly,
when you don't care what I say.

Don't dramatize concern.
I'm no extra in your show.
And don't ask how I feel,
you don't really want to know.

Part Two

I Can't Tell You

I can't tell you all I know.
I can't show you all I feel.
But there is much that I could say.
I could make your heart stand still.

Pain has grown so great in me,
pressing in on every side,
hauls me from my hiding place
takes me for a frenzied ride.

I can't tell you all I know.
I can't tell you what I feel,
but I promise if I did,
I could make your heart stand still.

Locked In

Affirmation

Sometimes people hang around.
Just to knock you to the ground.
Minimizing what you do.
Doubtful you can follow through.
Just believe the things you see.
Internalize the victory.
Reinvent the circumstance.
Seize the moment,
take the chance.
Don't endorse the wicked lie.
Grant yourself the right to try.
If they should say you can't achieve,
force yourself to disbelieve.
Jah has granted you this earth.
No mere man can judge your worth.
Once you're standing proud and tall,
you won't hear their words at all.

Part Two

Dilemma

Forgive and forget,
the Bible says.
And don't you hold no grudge.
Forgive and forget,
the Bible says
and let the MASTER judge.
Forgive and forget,
that's hard to do.
I guess I'd better pray.
Cause I gotta forgive
and I gotta forget,
before the judgment day.

Locked In

Attitude

It's a curious thing
how attitude shapes us.
It makes or it breaks us.
It scolds or it molds us.
Depletes or extols us.
It even compels us to feel what it tells us.
It's good or it's bad.
Makes us happy or sad.
And though it can school us,
it's been known to fool us.
Bad attitude…a terrible thing.
When it's nourished, it cheats us.
And so often keeps us
from goals we pursue,
from confidence, too.
But when it's a friend
it demands that we fly.
It exposes our wings
so, we take to the sky.
It's a curious thing
how it programs our minds.
It ruthlessly binds us
'til slavery confines us.
In shackles we dwell
and truth never finds us.
But, if we're perceptive,
in one shining hour
we can make our minds over,
and harness the power.
Eradicate dirges.
Commission a choir.

Part Two

Commit hurtful urges
to brimstone and fire.
Fine-tune each emotion.
Relinquish the fear.
Try to learn one life-lesson for every year.
Be conscience of danger
while seeking the good.
And walk in the footprints
where others have stood.
Strong forces inside you desire to achieve.
Just keep facing forward and always believe.

Locked In

Forgiveness

Nobody will understand,
so this is just for you and me.
Let me take your trembling hand,
and show you where I've come to be.
Misery and tears and pain,
fear and disbelief,
are images that cloud my brain
with hopelessness and grief.
These emotions blanket me
like storm clouds hide the sun.
But my heart is remembering,
before the pain had come.
And you were there, I recall.
You were there when I was small.
You picked me up when I would fall.
You taught me how to catch a ball.
You kept my clothes so clean and neat.
And worked real hard so we could eat.
You bought me pretty underwear.
You put ribbons in my hair.
Your silly stories made me laugh.
You made it fun to take a bath.
I know for sure you loved me then.
And what you gave was not pretend.
So, even when the music died,
my love for you remained alive.
You made mistakes that damaged me.
You closed your eyes and wouldn't see.
Shut your ears to stop the sound.
Gave me to that man you found.

Part Two

Though I can't negate the guilt,
I still feel the bond we built.
I see the sorrow in your eyes,
for laughter is a sad disguise.
And all the words you yearn to say,
just mock your lips then fade away.
So, lets not speak of ancient times.
I close my eyes to antique crimes.
Cause I do know you love me still.
You always have and always will.
So dry your eyes, I swear it's true.
I will always love you, too.
And my love has forgiven you.

Locked In

My Time to Heal

You've really got a lot of nerve.
I'm not surprised. I should have known.
And soon everyone will see
that you are ugly to the bone.

All I wanted was your love;
maybe an apology.
So why is there so much contempt
in every glance you throw at me?
I simply can't believe your nerve.
I can't believe your attitude.
I knew your eyes were tightly closed.
I didn't know your heart was lewd.

The act itself was bad enough.
The lie has pierced me deeper still.
But I'll just leave you to your lie.
This is my time.
My time to heal.

Part Two

Closure

I saw Mama yesterday.

An informal family affair
brought me home again.
Back to the warm and cozy house of horrors,
that darkened my childhood.

With a practiced smile,
I stepped into Mama's kitchen.

All eyes were on me.
And exuberant greetings flew my way,
but my eyes were riveted to the small, benign figure
of my mother.

Mama has always been physically small,
but her essence had been so large
that it tended to crowd a room.

The potency of that essence, her presence,
was now conspicuously absent.

But Mama met my gaze,
and when her eyes adhered to mine,
I read the cryptic lexis of emotion written there.

I saw pain
and some inscrutable fear.
I saw longing
and troubling questions that betrayed her smile
and saddened her eyes.

Locked In

I saw a prayer there, an entreaty,
whose hands reached out to me.

I saw the genesis of evolution
and I knew that,
in this crowded room of free flowing love,
there was only Mama and me,
and the plausible prelude
to the book of our genesis.

I can't wear my mother's shoes
or walk the paths her life decreed
or understand the things she did
or the things she did not do.

But I know that she knows, that harm was done
and how she failed her little ones.

And I know I may never hear the words.
They may not survive the trip from her heart,
or scale the wall of her pride.
But I will survive this deep slumber we've shared.
And if she survives and awakens
and if she turns her face to the sun,
she'll come to know the brilliance of love.

I have no more stones to cast
and no desire to cast them.
Because…

Part Two

I saw Mama yesterday.
I flowed into her arms
and she held on tight,
and she kissed my cheek.

I felt the frailness of her bones.
And with nothingness, she filled my arms.
There was no plump flesh,
to cushion me;
nothing to pad her fragile form.

But I was in my mother's arms
and found a vague contentment there.

It dawned on me, that I was home.
And I found that I could linger there.
I'd made the lengthy journey home,
and drove the demons from their lair.

This is not a perfect place.
It never was.
Can't ever be.
But oh, how good the feeling was.

Being home again.

Locked In

Healing

There's too much to do and not enough time.
Places to go and pleasures to find.
I'm never alone, for friendships abound.
And the voices I hear are benevolent sounds.

Once I was empty, my poem didn't rhyme.
I traveled alone; an all-uphill climb.
Time was a dream that slipped through my hands.
I had no great desires or pressing demands.

In a coffin of darkness where night never ends,
T.V. was solace and sleep was my friend.
Now, I beckon the light and bask in the sun.
I'm not finished with life; I've just begun.

And though sometimes I'm weary,
exhausted and frayed,
my soul is revived,
cause the game is well played.

My spirit is something!
This day is good!
We've done more with ourselves
than we dreamed that we could!

What is Dissociative Identity Disorder (DID)?

Dissociative Identity Disorder (DID), formerly called Multiple Personality Disorder, is a highly evolved survival mechanism acquired by some individuals as they cope with severe and prolonged trauma, abuse, and fear.

Dissociation is a mental process, which produces a lack of connection in a person's thoughts, memories, feelings, actions, or sense of identity. During the period of time when a person is dissociating, certain information is not associated with other information as it normally would be. For example, during a traumatic experience, a person may dissociate the memory of the place and circumstances of the trauma from his ongoing memory, resulting in a temporary mental escape from the fear and pain of the trauma and, in some cases, a memory gap surrounding the experience. Because this process can produce changes in memory, people who frequently dissociate often find their senses of personal history and identity are affected.

Most clinicians believe that dissociation exists on a continuum of severity. This continuum reflects a wide range of experiences and/or symptoms. At one end are mild dissociative experiences common to most people, such as daydreaming, highway hypnosis, or "getting lost" in a book or movie, all of which involve "losing touch" with conscious awareness of one's immediate surroundings.

At the other extreme is complex, chronic dissociation, such as in cases of Dissociative Disorders, which may result in serious impairment or inability to function.

Some people with Dissociative Disorders can hold highly responsible jobs, contributing to society in a variety of professions, the arts, and public service -- appearing to function normally to coworkers, neighbors, and others with whom they interact daily.

How Does A Dissociative Disorder Develop?

When faced with overwhelmingly traumatic situations from which there is no physical escape, a child may resort to "going away" in his or her head. Children typically use this ability as an extremely effective defense against acute physical and emotional pain, or anxious anticipation of that pain. By this dissociative process, thoughts, feelings, memories, and perceptions of the traumatic experiences can be separated off psychologically, allowing the child to function as if the trauma had not occurred.

Dissociative Disorders are often referred to as a highly creative survival technique because they allow individuals enduring "hopeless" circumstances to preserve some areas of healthy functioning. Over time, however, for a child who has been repeatedly physically and sexually assaulted, defensive dissociation becomes reinforced and conditioned. Because the dissociative escape is so effective, children who are very practiced at it may automatically use it whenever they feel threatened or anxious -- even if the anxiety-producing situation is not extreme or abusive. Often, even after the traumatic circumstances are long past, the left-over pattern of defensive dissociation remains. Chronic defensive dissociation may lead to serious dysfunction in work, social, and daily activities.

Repeated dissociation may result in a series of separate entities, or mental states, which may eventually take on identities of their own. These entities may become the internal "personality states" of a DID system. Changing between these states of consciousness is often described as "switching."

Can Dissociative Disorders Be Cured?

Yes. Dissociative Disorders are highly responsive to individual psychotherapy, or "talk therapy," as well as to a range of other treatment modalities, including medications, hypnotherapy, and adjunctive therapies such as art or movement therapy. In fact, among comparably severe psychiatric disorders, Dissociative Disorders may be the condition that carries the best prognosis if proper treatment is undertaken and completed. The course of treatment is long-term, intensive, and invariably painful, as it generally involves remembering and reclaiming the dissociated traumatic experiences. Nevertheless, individuals with Dissociative Disorders have been successfully treated by therapists of all professional backgrounds working in a variety of settings.

How Do I Get More Information?

For information on Dissociative Identity Disorders (DID) we recommend the contacting The Sidran Institute. Sidran helps people understand, manage, and treat dissociative and traumatic stress conditions. They are a national nonprofit organization and one of the nation's leading providers of traumatic stress education, publications, and resources.

The Sidran Institute
200 E. Joppa Road, Suite 207
Towson, MD 21286 USA
Phone: 410-825-8888
Web: www.sidran.org

This information is provided courtesy of the Sidran Institute

Thank You

The Culture Connection is proud to donate a portion of the proceeds from Locked In to Women For Women International.

Women for Women International supports women in war-torn regions with financial and emotional aid, job-skills training, rights education and small business assistance so they can rebuild their lives. To find out how you can help contact them at:

Women for Women International
4455 Connecticut Avenue, Suite 200
Washington, DC 20008
www.womenforwomen.org

Please visit our website at
www.thecultureconnection.com
to see our many services and other exciting titles.

Look for more titles coming soon including:

Jacob Daddy
Grasshopper
Hopper's Big Move
Lily and the Big Italian Wedding
Lily and the Lost Identity
Lily and the Little Brother Bother

www.ingramcontent.com/pod-product-compliance
Lightning Source LLC
Chambersburg PA
CBHW031250290426
44109CB00012B/522